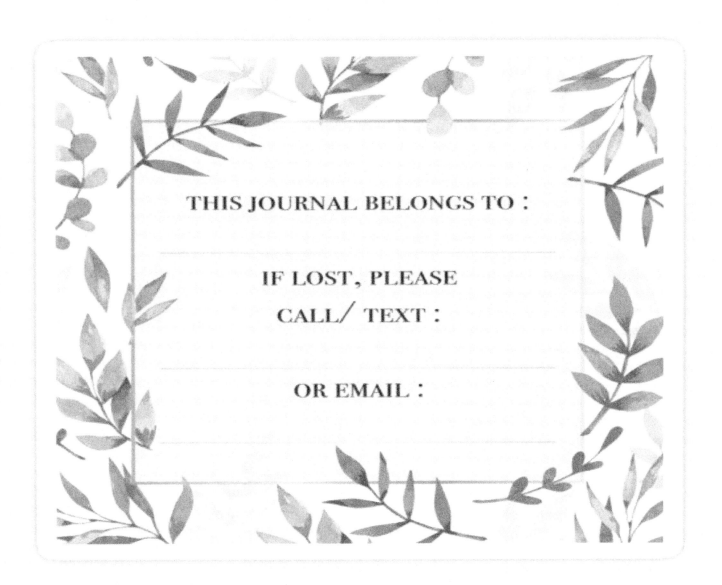

THIS JOURNAL BELONGS TO :

IF LOST, PLEASE

CALL/ TEXT :

OR EMAIL :

DATE

_____ / _____ / _____

Character is doing the right thing when nobody's looking.
J.C. Watts

What do we all have in common besides our genes that makes us human?

_____

_____

_____

Who do you sometimes compare yourself to?

_____

_____

_____

What's the most sensible thing you've ever heard someone say?

_____

_____

_____

DATE

_____ / _____ / _____

Not all those who wander are lost.
J.R. R. Tolkein

If the average human lifespan was 40 years, how would you live your life differently?

_____

_____

_____

What life lesson did you learn the hard way?

_____

_____

_____

What do you wish you spent more time doing five years ago?

_____

_____

_____

DATE

_____ / _____ / _____

There is no substitute for hard work.
Thomas Edison

If you had a friend who spoke to you in the same way that you speak to yourself, how long would you allow him to be your friend?

_____

_____

_____

Do you ask enough questions or do you settle for what you know?

_____

_____

_____

Who do you love and what are you doing about it?

_____

_____

_____

DATE

_____ / _____ / _____

Well done is better than well said.
Benjamin Franklin

What's a belief that you hold with which many people disagree?

_____

_____

_____

What can you do today that you were not capable of a year ago?

_____

_____

_____

Do you think crying is a sign of weakness or strength?

_____

_____

_____

DATE

_____ / _____ / _____

The worst loneliness is not to be comfortable with yourself.
Mark Twain

What would you do different if you knew nobody would judge you?

_____

_____

_____

Do you celebrate the things you do have?

_____

_____

_____

What is the difference between living and existing?

_____

_____

_____

DATE

_____ / _____ / _____

I may not have gone where I intended to go, but I think I have ended up where I needed to be.
Douglas Adams

If not now, then when?

_____

_____

_____

Have you done anything lately worth remembering?

_____

_____

_____

What does your joy look like today?

_____

_____

_____

DATE

_____ / _____ / _____

The best way to get started is to quit talking and begin doing.
Walt Disney

Is it possible to lie without saying a word?

_____

_____

_____

Which activities make you lose track of time?

_____

_____

_____

If you had to teach something, what would you teach?

_____

_____

_____

DATE

_____ / _____ / _____

If you are working on something that you really care about, you don't have to be pushed. The vision pulls you.

Steve Jobs

What would you regret not fully doing, being or having in your life?

_____

_____

_____

Are you holding onto something that you need to let go of?

_____

_____

_____

When you are 80-years-old, what will matter to you the most?

_____

_____

_____

DATE

_____ / _____ / _____

Many of life's failures are people who did not realize how close they were to success when they gave up.
Thomas Edison

How old would you be if you didn't know how old you are?

_____

_____

_____

Would you break the law to save a loved one?

_____

_____

_____

What makes you smile?

_____

_____

_____

DATE

_____ / _____ / _____

The dictionary is the only place where success comes before work.
Mark Twain

What is important enough to go to war over?

_____

_____

_____

Which is worse, failing or never trying?

_____

_____

_____

When was the last time you listened to the sound of your breathing?

_____

_____

_____

DATE

_____ / _____ / _____

The odds of hitting your target go up dramatically when you aim at it.

Mal Pancoast

What's something you know you do differently than most people?

_____

_____

_____

What does 'The American Dream' mean to you?

_____

_____

_____

Would you rather be a worried genius or a joyful simpleton?

_____

_____

_____

DATE

_____ / _____ / _____

Success if getting what you want. Happiness is wanting what you get.
Dale Carnegie

What is the most desirable trait another person can possess?

_____

_____

_____

What are you most grateful for?

_____

_____

_____

Is stealing to feed a starving child wrong?

_____

_____

_____

DATE

_____ / _____ / _____

Nobody can bring you peace but yourself.
Ralph Waldo Emerson

What do you want most?

_____

_____

_____

Are you worried about doing things right, or doing the right things?

_____

_____

_____

What has life taught you recently?

_____

_____

_____

DATE

_____ / _____ / _____

Try and fail, but don't fail to try.
Stephen Kaggwa

If we learn from our mistakes, why are we always so afraid to make a mistake?

_____

_____

_____

Where do you find inspiration?

_____

_____

_____

Can you describe your life in a six word sentence?

_____

_____

_____

DATE

_____ / _____ / _____

A man cannot be comfortable without his own approval.
Mark Twain

If you could instill one piece of advice in a newborn baby's mind, what advice would you give?

_____

_____

_____

What impact do you want to leave on the world?

_____

_____

_____

What is the most defining moment of your life thus far?

_____

_____

_____

DATE

_____ / _____ / _____

The greatest barrier to success is the fear of failure.
Eriksson

If we learn from our mistakes, why are we always so afraid to make a mistake?

_____

_____

_____

In the haste of your daily life, what are you not seeing?

_____

_____

_____

What lifts your spirits when life gets you down?

_____

_____

_____

DATE

_____ / _____ / _____

To be great, is to be misunderstood.
Ralph Waldo Emerson

If life is so short, why do we do so many things we don't like and like so many things we don't do?

_____

_____

_____

Have you ever regretted something you did not say or do?

_____

_____

_____

Has your greatest fear ever come true?

_____

_____

_____

DATE

_____ / _____ / _____

Every saint has a past. Every sinner has a future.
Oscar Wilde

When is it time to stop calculating risk and rewards and just do what you know is right?

_____

_____

_____

Why do we think of others the most when they're gone?

_____

_____

_____

What is your most beloved childhood memory?

_____

_____

_____

DATE

_____ / _____ / _____

There is no beauty without some strangeness.
Edgar Allen Poe

If you had the chance to go back in time and change one thing would you do it?

_____

_____

_____

Is it more important to love or be loved?

_____

_____

_____

If it all came back around to you, would it help you or hurt you?

_____

_____

_____

DATE

_____ / _____ / _____

Ignorance more frequently begets confidence than does knowledge.
Charles Darwin

If a doctor gave you five years to live, what would you try to accomplish?

_____

_____

_____

What is the difference between falling in love and being in love?

_____

_____

_____

Who do you think stands between you and happiness?

_____

_____

_____

DATE

_____ / _____ / _____

I am not what happened to me. I am what I choose to become
Carl Jung

Can there be happiness without sadness? Pleasure without pain? Peace without war?

_____

_____

_____

What gives your life meaning?

_____

_____

_____

What is the simplest truth you can express in words?

_____

_____

_____

DATE

_____ / _____ / _____

To live is the rarest thing in the world. Most people exist, that is all.

Oscar Wilde

What is the difference between innocence and ignorance?

_____

_____

_____

Is there such a thing as perfect?

_____

_____

_____

What does it mean to be human?

_____

_____

_____

DATE

_____ / _____ / _____

Live each day as if your life had just begun.
Johann Wolfgang

To what degree have you actually controlled the course your life has taken?

_____

_____

_____

What do you love most about yourself?

_____

_____

_____

Where would you most like to go and why?

_____

_____

_____

DATE

_____ / _____ / _____

The mind is everything. What you think, you become
Buddha

Is it more important to do what you love or to Love what you are doing?

_____

_____

_____

What do you imagine yourself doing ten years from now?

_____

_____

_____

What is your happiest childhood memory?

_____

_____

_____

DATE

_____ / _____ / _____

Life is too short to spend another day at war with yourself
Confucius

What's the one thing you'd like others to remember about you at the end of your life?

_____

_____

_____

Do you own your things or do your things own you?

_____

_____

_____

What do you have that you cannot live without?

_____

_____

_____

DATE

_____ / _____ / _____

Nothing haunts us like the things we don't say.
Mitch Albom

If you looked into the heart of your enemy, what do you think you would find that is different from what is in your own heart?

_____

_____

_____

When you close your eyes what do you see?

_____

_____

_____

What sustains you on a daily basis?

_____

_____

_____

DATE

_____ / _____ / _____

We ARE our choices.
J.P. Sartre

What small act of kindness were you once shown that you will never forget?

_____

_____

_____

What are your top five personal values?

_____

_____

_____

Why must you love someone enough to let them go?

_____

_____

_____

DATE

_____ / _____ / _____

Most people would learn from their mistakes, if they weren't so busy denying them.

Harold J. Smith

Do you ever celebrate the green lights?

_____

_____

_____

What personal prisons have you built out of fears?

_____

_____

_____

What one thing have you not done that you really want to do?

_____

_____

_____

DATE

_____ / _____ / _____

Make is simple, but significant.
Don Draper

Would you rather lose all of your old memories or never be able to make new ones?

_____

_____

_____

Why are you, you?

_____

_____

_____

If you haven't achieved it yet what do you have to lose?

_____

_____

_____

DATE

_____ / _____ / _____

Before you embark on a journey of revenge, dig two graves.
Confucius

What three words would you use to describe the last three months of your life?

_____

_____

_____

What is your number one goal for the next six months?

_____

_____

_____

Would you ever give up your life to save someone else?

_____

_____

_____

DATE

_____ / _____ / _____

If not us, who? If not now, when?
John F. Kennedy

How do you deal with someone in a position of power who wants you to fail?

_____

_____

_____

Are you happy with yourself?

_____

_____

_____

What is the meaning of 'peace' to you?

_____

_____

_____

DATE

_____ / _____ / _____

I'm rarely bored alone; I am often bored in groups and crowds.
Laurie Halgoe

Is it ever right to do the wrong thing? Is it ever wrong to do the right thing?

_____

_____

_____

What are three moral rules you will never break?

_____

_____

_____

What does it mean to allow another person to truly love you?

_____

_____

_____

DATE

_____ / _____ / _____

When you complain, you make yourself the victim. Leave the situation, change the situation, or accept it. All else is madness.
Eckhart Tolle

Who or what do you think of when you think of love?

_____

_____

_____

What would you not give up for $1,000,000 in cash?

_____

_____

_____

When do you feel most like yourself?

_____

_____

_____

DATE

_____ / _____ / _____

What is love? Love is absence of judgement.
Dalai Lama

What is the most important thing you could do right now in your personal life?

_____

_____

_____

When you help someone do you ever think, "What's in it for me?"

_____

_____

_____

What is your greatest challenge?

_____

_____

_____

DATE

_____ / _____ / _____

Be a voice, not an echo.
Albert Einstein

How do you know when it's time to continue holding on or time to let
go?

_____

_____

_____

How do you define success?

_____

_____

_____

If I could grant you one wish what would you wish for?

_____

_____

_____

DATE

_____ / _____ / _____

When I let go of what I am, I become what I might be.
Lao Tzu

If you could ask one person, alive or dead, only one question, who would you ask and what would you ask?

_____

_____

_____

What have you read online recently that inspired you?

_____

_____

_____

Why do religions that advocate unity divide the human race?

_____

_____

_____

DATE

_____ / _____ / _____

If it wasn't for failures, I wouldn't know what strength looked like.
Byron Pulsifer

If you provided a chance to live your life again, what would be your first priority?

_____

_____

_____

What can money not buy?

_____

_____

_____

If you left this life tomorrow, how would you be remembered?

_____

_____

_____

DATE

_____ / _____ / _____

The joy in life is to be used for a purpose. I want to be all used up when I die.

George Bernard Shaw

Beyond the titles that others have given you, who are you?

_____

_____

_____

Is it possible to know the truth without challenging it first?

_____

_____

_____

What makes everyone smile?

_____

_____

_____

DATE

_____ / _____ / _____

He who angers you, conquers you.
Elizabeth Kenny

What is the one thing you would most like to change about the world?

_____

_____

_____

What do you owe yourself?

_____

_____

_____

What would your 'priceless' Mastercard-style commercial be?

_____

_____

_____

DATE

_____ / _____ / _____

When you have a dream, you've got to grab it and never let go.
Carol Burnett

If happiness was the national currency, what kind of work would make you rich?

_____

_____

_____

Can you think of a time when impossible became possible?

_____

_____

_____

Why do you matter?

_____

_____

_____

DATE

_____ / _____ / _____

Nothing is impossible. The word itself says 'I'm possible.
Audrey Hepburn

If your life was a novel, what would be the title and how would your story end?

_____

_____

_____

How have you changed in the last three years?

_____

_____

_____

What are you sure of in your life?

_____

_____

_____

DATE

_____ / _____ / _____

There is nothing impossible to they who will try.
Alexander the Great

What's the difference between settling for things and accepting the way things are?

_____

_____

_____

When you think of 'home,' what, specifically, do you think of?

_____

_____

_____

How many of your friends would you trust with your life?

_____

_____

_____

DATE

_____ / _____ / _____

The bad news is time flies. The good news is you're the pilot.
Michael Altshuler

If someone could tell you the exact day and time you are going to die, would you want them to tell you?

_____

_____

_____

What's your definition of heaven?

_____

_____

_____

What is your most prized possession?

_____

_____

_____

DATE

_____ / _____ / _____

Life has got all those twists and turns. You've got to hold on tight and off you go.
Nicole Kidman

How would you describe yourself in one sentence?

_____

_____

_____

What stands between you and happiness?

_____

_____

_____

What makes a person beautiful?

_____

_____

_____

DATE

_____ / _____ / _____

You define your own life. Don't let other people write your script.
Oprah Winfrey

How do you find the strength to do what you know in your heart is right?

_____

_____

_____

Is there ever a time when giving up makes sense?

_____

_____

_____

What makes you proud?

_____

_____

_____

DATE

_____ / _____ / _____

Spread love everywhere you go.
Mother Teresa

How short would your life have to be before you would start living
differently today?

_____

_____

_____

Where do you find peace?

_____

_____

_____

When have you worked hard and loved every minute of it?

_____

_____

_____

DATE

_____ / _____ / _____

You can be everything. You can be the infinite amount of things that people are.

Kesha

Is it better to have loved and lost or to have never loved at all?

_____

_____

_____

What would you do if you made a mistake and somebody died?

_____

_____

_____

Who do you trust and why?

_____

_____

_____

DATE

_____ / _____ / _____

Belief creates the actual fact.
William James

If you could live one day of your life over again, what day would you choose?

_____

_____

_____

When does silence convey more meaning than words?

_____

_____

_____

How do you spend the majority of your free time?

_____

_____

_____

DATE

_____ / _____ / _____

No matter what people tell you, words and ideas can change the world.

Robin Williams

Who do you think of first when you think of success?

_____

_____

_____

What did you want to be when you grew up?

_____

_____

_____

How will today matter in five years from now?

_____

_____

_____

DATE

_____ / _____ / _____

It is during our darkest moments that we must focus to see the light.

Aristotle

How have you helped someone else recently?

_____

_____

_____

What is your greatest skill?

_____

_____

_____

Do you see to believe or believe to see?

_____

_____

_____

DATE

_____ / _____ / _____

Not having the best situation, but seeing the best in your situation is the key to happiness.

Marie Forleo

How are you pursuing your dreams right now?

_____

_____

_____

What's the next big step you need to take?

_____

_____

_____

Who do you dream about?

_____

_____

_____

DATE

_____ / _____ / _____

Believe you can and you're halfway there.
Theodore Roosevelt

If you could live the next 24 hours and then erase it and start over just once, what would you do?

_____

_____

_____

What do you have trouble seeing clearly in your mind?

_____

_____

_____

What are you looking forward to?

_____

_____

_____

DATE

_____ / _____ / _____

Weaknesses are just strengths in the wrong environment.
Marianne Cantwell

What word best describes the way you've spent the last month of your life?

_____

_____

_____

What is the number one thing you want to accomplish before you die?

_____

_____

_____

When is love a weakness?

_____

_____

_____

DATE

_____ / _____ / _____

Silence is the last thing the world will ever hear from me.
Marlee Matlin

If today was the last day of your life, would you want to do what you are about to do today?

_____

_____

_____

What has been the most terrifying moment of your life thus far?

_____

_____

_____

Who is the strongest person you know?

_____

_____

_____

DATE

_____ / _____ / _____

Learning how to be still, to really be still and let life happen—that stillness becomes a radiance.

Morgan Freeman

Is the reward worth the risk?

_____

_____

_____

For you personally, what makes today worth living?

_____

_____

_____

What have you done in the last year that makes you proud?

_____

_____

_____

DATE

_____ / _____ / _____

All you need is the plan, the road map, and the courage to press on to your destination.

Earl Nightingale

What did you learn recently that changed the way you live?

_____

_____

_____

What is your fondest memory from the past three years?

_____

_____

_____

What are the primary components of a happy life?

_____

_____

_____

DATE

_____ / _____ / _____

Try to be a rainbow in someone's cloud.
Maya Angelou

With the resources you have right now, what can you do to bring yourself closer to your goal?

_____

_____

_____

How would the world be different if you were never born?

_____

_____

_____

What is your favorite song and why?

_____

_____

_____

DATE

_____ / _____ / _____

We must let go of the life we have planned, so as to accept the one that is waiting for us.

Joseph Campbell

What are your top three priorities?

_____

_____

_____

Why do we idolize sports players?

_____

_____

_____

What is the nicest thing someone has ever done for you?

_____

_____

_____

Real change, enduring change, happens one step at a time.
Ruth Bader Ginsburg

If today was the last day of your life, who would you call and what would you tell them?

_____

_____

_____

What do you see when you look into the future?

_____

_____

_____

What makes you angry? Why?

_____

_____

_____

DATE

_____ / _____ / _____

Wake up determined, go to bed satisfied.
Dwayne Johnson

If you could take a single photograph of your life, what would it look like?

_____

_____

_____

What is the most valuable life lesson you learned from your parents?

_____

_____

_____

What does love feel like?

_____

_____

_____

DATE

_____ / _____ / _____

Nobody built like you, you design yourself.
Jay-Z

If you could go back in time and tell a younger version of yourself one thing, what would you tell?

_____

_____

_____

What are your favorite simple pleasures?

_____

_____

_____

What do you do to deliberately impress others?

_____

_____

_____

DATE

_____ / _____ / _____

Live your beliefs and you can turn the world around.
Henry David Thoreau

If you were forced to keep a single physical possession of your life, what would you put in backpack?

_____

_____

_____

What will you never do?

_____

_____

_____

Excluding romantic relationships, who do you love?

_____

_____

_____

DATE

_____ / _____ / _____

Life is like riding a bicycle. To keep your balance, you must keep moving.

Albert Einstein

What is your earliest childhood memory?

_____

_____

_____

What book has had the greatest influence on your life?

_____

_____

_____

What three questions do you wish you knew the answers to?

_____

_____

_____

DATE

_____ / _____ / _____

Don't try to lessen yourself for the world; let the world catch up to you.

Beyoncé

What is the greatest peer pressure you've ever felt?

_____

_____

_____

What's the biggest lie you once believed was true?

_____

_____

_____

In your lifetime, what have you done that hurt someone else?

_____

_____

_____

DATE

_____ / _____ / _____

I have learned over the years that when one's mind is made up, this diminishes fear; knowing what must be done does away with fear.

Rosa Parks

What's the best part of growing older?

_____

_____

_____

What's been on your mind most lately?

_____

_____

_____

What do you think is worth waiting for?

_____

_____

_____

DATE

_____ / _____ / _____

I've noticed when I fear something, if I just end up doing it, I'm grateful in the end.

Colleen Hoover

What chances do you wish you had taken?

_____

_____

_____

Where else would you like to live? Why?

_____

_____

_____

What motivates you to go to work each day?

_____

_____

_____

DATE

_____ / _____ / _____

When you've seen beyond yourself, then you may find, peace of mind is waiting there.

George Harrison

What do you wish you had done differently?

_____

_____

_____

What is your greatest strength and your greatest weakness?

_____

_____

_____

When was the last time you lied? What did you lie about?

_____

_____

_____

DATE

_____ / _____ / _____

What you get by achieving your goals is not as important as what you become by achieving your goals.
Zig Ziglar

What made you smile this week?

_____

_____

_____

What do you do with the majority of your money?

_____

_____

_____

What motivates you to be your best?

_____

_____

_____

DATE

_____ / _____ / _____

Out of the mountain of despair, a stone of hope.
Martin Luther King, Jr

Do you remember when was the last time you lost your temper?
About what?

_____

_____

_____

What will you never give up on?

_____

_____

_____

When you look into the past, what do you miss the most?

_____

_____

_____

DATE

_____ / _____ / _____

You are never too old to set another goal or to dream a new dream.
C.S. Lewis

If you had to move 3000 miles away, what one thing would you miss the most?

_____

_____

_____

What makes you uncomfortable?

_____

_____

_____

What is the most spontaneous thing you've ever done?

_____

_____

_____

DATE

_____ / _____ / _____

I believe that if you'll just stand up and go, life will open up for you.
Something just motivates you to keep moving.

Tina Turner

What worries you about the future?

_____

_____

_____

Do you like the city or town you live in? Why or why not?

_____

_____

_____

What's the best part of being you?

_____

_____

_____

DATE

_____ / _____ / _____

How wild it was, to let it be.
Cheryl Strayed

What one 'need' and one 'want' will you strive to achieve in the next twelve months?

_____

_____

_____

How would you describe the past year of your life in one sentence?

_____

_____

_____

What do you do to relieve stress?

_____

_____

_____

DATE

_____ / _____ / _____

The simple act of listening to someone and making them feel as if they have truly been heard is a most treasured gift.

L. A. Villafane

What is your happiest memory?

_____

_____

_____

What is your saddest memory?

_____

_____

_____

What would you like to change (about yourself)?

_____

_____

_____

DATE

_____ / _____ / _____

You have to be where you are to get where you need to go.
Amy Poehler

What life lessons did you have to experience firsthand before you fully understood them?

_____

_____

_____

How many people do you love?

_____

_____

_____

What's the best decision you've ever made?

_____

_____

_____

DATE

_____ / _____ / _____

Don't be afraid. Because you're going to be afraid. But remember when you become afraid, just don't be afraid.
Joan Jett

What's your favorite true story that you enjoy sharing with others?

_____

_____

_____

Right now, at this moment, what do you want most?

_____

_____

_____

What are you waiting for? How are you writing your life's story?

_____

_____

_____

DATE

_____ / _____ / _____

We need to take risks. We need to go broke. We need to prove them wrong, simply by not giving up.

Awkwafina

What makes love last?

_____

_____

_____

What good comes from suffering?

_____

_____

_____

What's the most important lesson you've learned in the last year?

_____

_____

_____

DATE

_____ / _____ / _____

It is never too late to be what you might have been.
George Eliot

Based on you current daily actions and routines, where would you expect to be in five years?

_____

_____

_____

What was your last major accomplishment?

_____

_____

_____

Through all of life's twists and turns who has been there for you?

_____

_____

_____

DATE

_____ / _____ / _____

The only limit to our realization of tomorrow will be our doubts today.

Franklin Delano Roosevelt

What or who has been distracting you?

_____

_____

_____

What are you looking forward to in the upcoming week?

_____

_____

_____

Who is your mentor and what have you learned from them?

_____

_____

_____

DATE

_____ / _____ / _____

You do not find the happy life. You make it.
Camilla Eyring Kimball

When you look back over the past month, what single moment stands out?

_____

_____

_____

What are you uncertain about?

_____

_____

_____

What do you think about when you lie awake in bed?

_____

_____

_____

DATE

_____ / _____ / _____

Definitions belong to the definers, not the defined.
Toni Morrison

When you have a random hour of free time, what do you usually want to do?

_____

_____

_____

What's something most people don't know about you?

_____

_____

_____

What makes you weird?

_____

_____

_____

DATE

_____ / _____ / _____

You must find the place inside yourself where nothing is impossible.

Deepak Chopra

If you could relive yesterday what would you do differently?

_____

_____

_____

What do you do over and over again that you hate doing?

_____

_____

_____

What white lies do you often tell?

_____

_____

_____

DATE

_____ / _____ / _____

Whatever you think the world is withholding from you, you are withholding from the world.
Eckhart Tolle

What is the biggest change you have made in your life in last year?

_____

_____

_____

Whose life have you had the greatest impact on?

_____

_____

_____

What did life teach you yesterday?

_____

_____

_____

DATE

_____ / _____ / _____

Perfection is not attainable, but if we chase perfection we can catch excellence.

Vince Lombardi

Who impresses you?

_____

_____

_____

What have you done that you are not proud of?

_____

_____

_____

How would you spend your ideal day?

_____

_____

_____

DATE

_____ / _____ / _____

A lot of people are afraid to say what they want. That's why they don't get what they want.

Madonna

What is the one primary quality you look for in a significant other?

_____

_____

_____

What do you admire most about your mother and father?

_____

_____

_____

What is the best advice you have ever received?

_____

_____

_____

DATE

_____ / _____ / _____

We have to let go of who we think we should be and embrace what is.

Achea Redd

If you could live forever, would you want to? Why?

_____

_____

_____

What positive changes have you made in your life recently?

_____

_____

_____

Who makes you feel good about yourself?

_____

_____

_____

DATE

_____ / _____ / _____

Being vulnerable is a strength, not a weakness.
Selena Gomez

What is something you don't like to do that you are still really good at?

_____

_____

_____

What is your biggest regret?

_____

_____

_____

Which one of your responsibilities do you wish you could get rid of?

_____

_____

_____

DATE

_____ / _____ / _____

In order for the light to shine so brightly, the darkness must be present.

Sir Francis Bacon

What type of person angers you the most?

_____

_____

_____

What is missing in your life?

_____

_____

_____

What is your most striking physical attribute?

_____

_____

_____

DATE

_____ / _____ / _____

I don't look ahead. I'm right here with you. It's a good way to be.
Danny DeVito

If you could go back in time and change things, what would you change about the week that just passed?

_____

_____

_____

What has fear of failure stopped you from doing?

_____

_____

_____

Who would you like to please the most?

_____

_____

_____

DATE

_____ / _____ / _____

It ain't about how hard you hit. It's about how hard you can get hit and keep moving forward.

Sylvester Stallone

Who would you like to forgive?

_____

_____

_____

At what point during the last five years have you felt lost and alone?

_____

_____

_____

What do you want more of in your life?

_____

_____

_____

DATE

_____ / _____ / _____

I will not let anyone scare me out of my full potential.
Nicki Minaj

Would you rather your child be less attractive and extremely intelligent or extremely attractive and less intelligent?

_____

_____

_____

Who depends on you?

_____

_____

_____

Who has had the greatest impact on your life?

_____

_____

_____

DATE

_____ / _____ / _____

Trying to grow up is hurting. You make mistakes. You try to learn from them, and when you don't, it hurts even more.
Aretha Franklin

In one year from today, how do you think your life will be different?

_____

_____

_____

How have you sabotaged yourself in the past five years?

_____

_____

_____

Are you happy with where you are in your life? Why?

_____

_____

_____

DATE

_____ / _____ / _____

The power of imagination makes us infinite.
John Muir

Other than money, what else have you gained from your current job?

_____

_____

_____

Whom do you secretly envy? Why?

_____

_____

_____

In twenty years, what do you want to remember?

_____

_____

_____

DATE

_____ / _____ / _____

The only journey is the one within.
Rainer Maria Rilke

What is the most enjoyable thing your family has done together in the last three years?

_____

_____

_____

What are you most excited about in your life right now – today?

_____

_____

_____

What experience from this past year do you appreciate the most?

_____

_____

_____

DATE

_____ / _____ / _____

Embrace the glorious mess that you are.
Elizabeth Gilbert

How many hours of television do you watch in a week? A month? A year?

_____

_____

_____

What do you like most about your job?

_____

_____

_____

What do you dislike most about your job?

_____

_____

_____

DATE

_____ / _____ / _____

We become what we think about.
Earl Nightingale

What do you understand today about your life that you did not understand a year ago?

_____

_____

_____

What's something new you recently learned about yourself?

_____

_____

_____

What is the biggest obstacle that stands in your way right now?

_____

_____

_____

DATE

_____ / _____ / _____

Believe you can and you're halfway there.
Theodore Roosevelt

In one sentence, how would you describe your relationship with your mother?

_____

_____

_____

What was most defining moment in your life during this past year?

_____

_____

_____

What makes you feel secure?

_____

_____

_____

DATE

_____ / _____ / _____

Everything you've ever wanted is on the other side of fear.
George Addair

What simple gesture have you recently witnessed that renewed your hope in humanity?

_____

_____

_____

What is your favorite sound?

_____

_____

_____

What are the top three qualities you look for in a friend?

_____

_____

_____

DATE

_____ / _____ / _____

You get what you give.
Jennifer Lopez

What's the number one change you need to make in your life in the next twelve months?

_____

_____

_____

What is your favorite smell?

_____

_____

_____

What recent memory makes you smile the most?

_____

_____

_____

DATE

_____ / _____ / _____

Your life only gets better when you get better.
Brian Tracy

What is one opportunity you believe you missed out on when you were younger?

_____

_____

_____

In one word, how would you describe your childhood?

_____

_____

_____

What celebrities do you admire? Why?

_____

_____

_____

DATE

_____ / _____ / _____

Happiness is not by chance, but by choice.
Jim Rohn

What music do you listen to to lift your spirits when you're feeling down?

_____

_____

_____

What is the number one motivator in your life right now?

_____

_____

_____

What was the last thing that made you laugh out loud?

_____

_____

_____

DATE

_____ / _____ / _____

We generate fears while we sit. We overcome them by action.
Dr. Henry Link

If I gave you $1000 and told you that you had to spend it today, what would you buy?

_____

_____

_____

What is your biggest pet peeve?

_____

_____

_____

When should you reveal a secret that you promised wouldn't reveal?

_____

_____

_____

DATE

_____ / _____ / _____

Today's accomplishments were yesterday's impossibilities.
Robert H. Schuller

When you meet someone for the very first time what do you want them to think about you?

_____

_____

_____

If you had to be someone else for one day, who would you be?

_____

_____

_____

Are you feeding your fears or your hopes and dreams?

_____

_____

_____

DATE

_____ / _____ / _____

You only live once, but if you do it right, once is enough.
Mae West

If you could choose one book as a mandatory read for all high school students, which book would you choose?

_____

_____

_____

When was the last time you tried something new?

_____

_____

_____

What gets you excited about life?

_____

_____

_____

DATE

_____ / _____ / _____

Light tomorrow with today!
Elizabeth Barrett Browning

When it's all said and done, will you have said more than you've done?

_____

_____

_____

Would you enjoy doing less work or more work?

_____

_____

_____

What would your message be for large group of people?

_____

_____

_____

DATE

_____ / _____ / _____

Speak less than you know; have more than you show.
William Shakespeare

What do you really love to do? Do you do it often? If you answer no, why not?

_____

_____

_____

What are you spending your money on?

_____

_____

_____

What is your favorite quote?

_____

_____

_____

DATE

_____ / _____ / _____

Education costs money. But then so does ignorance.
Sir Claus Moser

If you could spend 10 minutes with anyone, living or dead, who would it be? And why?

_____

_____

_____

What are your 5 most important values in life right now?

_____

_____

_____

Do you need any help to achieve your goals?

_____

_____

_____

Printed in Great Britain
by Amazon